Pip and Mits

By Sally Cowan

Tam pats Pip
at the pit.

Tap! Tap! Tap!

It is Tim and Mits.

Mits! Mits!

Mits is at the pit.

Pip! Pip!

Tim, is Pip at the pit?

Sit, Mits, sit!

CHECKING FOR MEANING

1. What is Tam doing at the start of the story? *(Literal)*

2. Where does Tam find Pip? *(Literal)*

3. Why do you think Mits was digging a hole in the pit? *(Inferential)*

EXTENDING VOCABULARY

Tam	Look at the word *Tam*. What sounds are in this word? Which sound is changed to turn *Tam* into *Tim*?
It	Look at the word *It*. Find a word in the book that ends in *-it*. Can you think of any other words that end with *-it*?
Tap	Look at the word *Tap* and think about what it means in the story. Can you think of another word that means the same as *Tap*?

MOVING BEYOND THE TEXT

1. What special features do rabbits have?

2. How are dogs like rabbits? How are they different?

3. What sorts of things might you find buried in a pit?

4. What can you use to dig with?

SPEED SOUNDS

| Mm | Ss | Aa | Pp | Ii | Tt |

PRACTICE WORDS

Tam

pats

Tap

at

pit

Pip

It

Tim

Sit

sit

Mits